Japanese Gardens Revisited

Photographs by KIICHI ASANO

Commentary by GISEI TAKAKUWA

English adaptation by Frank Davies & Hirokuni Kobatake

CHARLES E. TUTTLE COMPANY
Rutland · Vermont : Tokyo · Japan

Representatives

For Continental Europe:
BOXERBOOKS, INC., *Zurich*
For the British Isles:
PRENTICE-HALL INTERNATIONAL, INC., *London*
For Australasia:
PAUL FLESCH & CO., PTY. LTD., *Melbourne*
For Canada:
M. G. HURTIG, LTD., *Edmonton*

Published by the Charles E. Tuttle Company, Inc. of Rutland, Vermont & Tokyo, Japan with editorial offices at Suido 1-chome, 2-6, Bunkyo-ku, Tokyo; with the cooperation of Miṭsumura Suiko Shoin, publishers of the original Japanese version.

Library of Congress Catalog Card No. 72-88930
International Standard Book No. 0-8048 1047-8

First printing, 1973

Layout of plates by Susumu Masunaka
PRINTED IN JAPAN

Table·of Contents

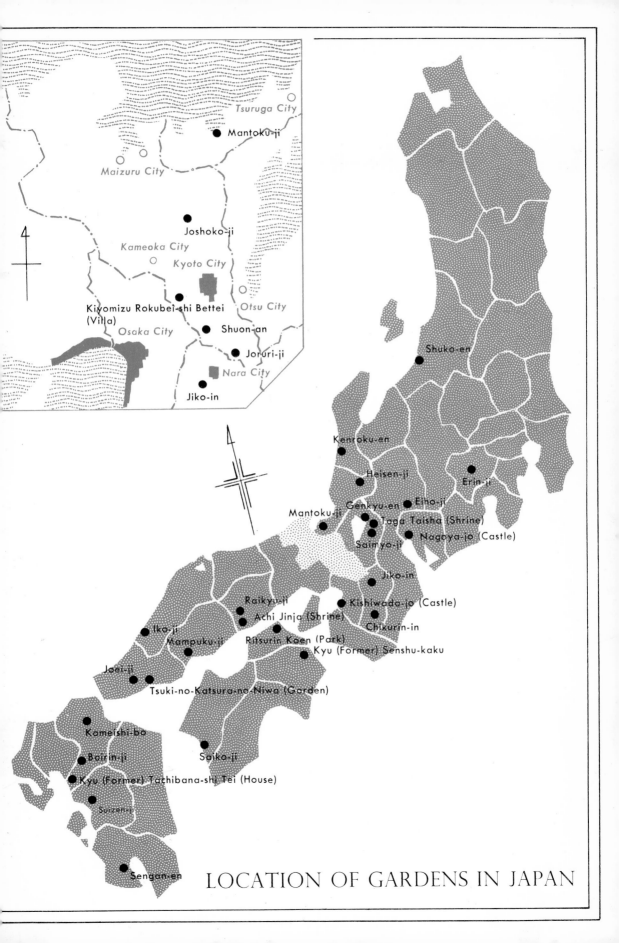

Tsuruga City

● Mantoku-ji

Maizuru City

● Joshoko-ji

Kameoka City

Kyoto City

Otsu City

Kiyomizu Rokubei-shi Bettei
(Villa)

Osaka City

● Shuon-an

Nara City

● Joruri-ji

● Jiko-in

Shuko-en ●

Kenroku-en ●

Heisen-ji ●

Erin-ji ●

Mantoku-ji ●

Genkyu-en ● Eiho-ji ●

Taga Taisha (Shrine) ●

Saimyo-ji ● Nagoya-jo (Castle) ●

Jiko-in ●

Raikyu-ji ●

Achi Jinja (Shrine) ●

Kishiwada-jo (Castle) ●

Chikurin-in ●

Iko-ji ●

Mampuku-ji ●

Ritsurin Koen (Park) ●

Kyu (Former) Senshu-kaku ●

Joei-ji ●

Tsuki-no-Katsura-no-Niwa (Garden)

Komeishi-bo ●

Bairin-ji ●

Kyu (Former) Tachibana-shi Tei (House) ●

Suizen-i ●

Saiko-ji ●

Sengan-en ●

LOCATION OF GARDENS IN JAPAN

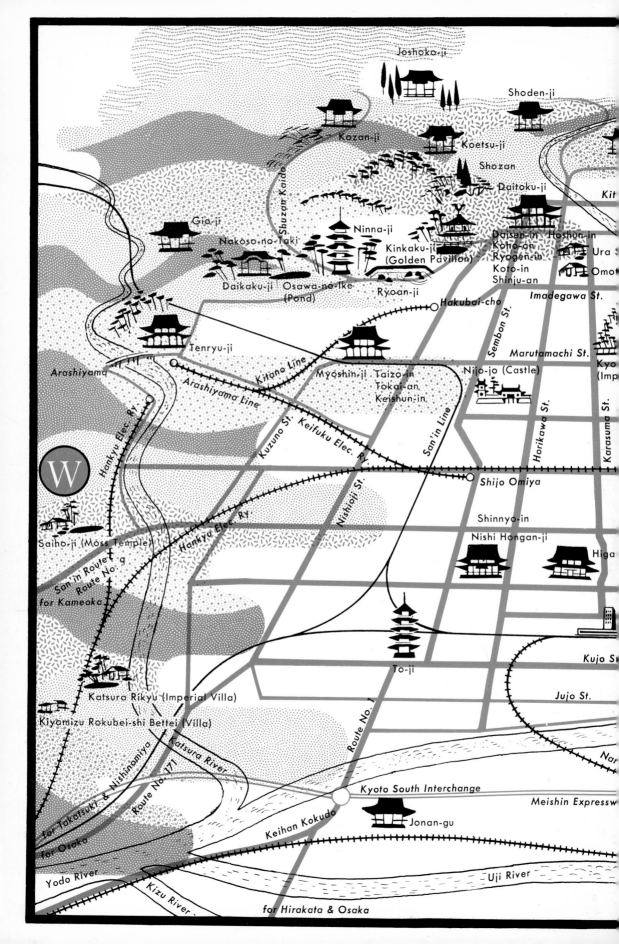

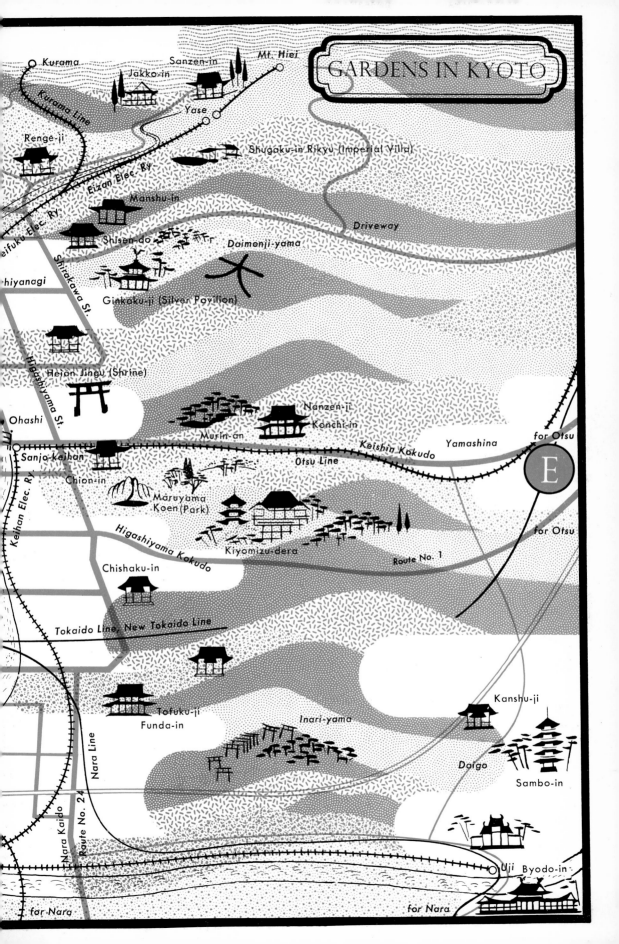

GARDENS IN KYOTO

Kurama

Jakko-in

Sanzen-in

Mt. Hiei

Kurama Line

Yase

Renge-ji

Shugaku-in Rikyu (Imperial Villa)

Eizan Elec. Ry.

Eifuku Elec. Ry.

Manshu-in

Driveway

Shisen-do

Daimonji-yama

hiyanagi

Shirakawa St.

Ginkaku-ji (Silver Pavilion)

Higashiyama St.

Heian Jingu (Shrine)

Ohashi

Nanzen-ji

Murin-an

Konchi-in

Yamashina

for Otsu

Keishin Kokudo

Sanjo-keihan

Otsu Line

E

Chion-in

for Otsu

Keihan Elec. Ry.

Maruyama Koen (Park)

Higashiyama Kokudo

Kiyomizu-dera

Route No. 1

Chishaku-in

Tokaido Line, New Tokaido Line

Kanshu-ji

Tofuku-ji

Inari-yama

Funda-in

Nara Line

Daigo

Route No. 24

Sambo-in

Nara Kaido

Uji Byodo-in

for Nara

for Nara

A Brief History of Japanese Gardens

The Natural Beauty of Pond-Gardens

Kyoyo-chi Pond, Ryoan-ji, Kyoto.
Kamakura period.

...wa Pond near Daikaku-ji, Kyoto.
...an period.

3

Kinkaku-ji (Golden Pavilion), Kyoto.
Muromachi period.

gon-chi Pond, Lower Garden, Saiho-ji (Moss Temple), Kyoto.
uromachi period.

Main buildings and Front Garden, Katsura Imperial Villa, Kyoto.
Early Edo period.

Kyu Ni-no-Maru garden, Nijo Castle, Kyoto. Early Edo period.

Ritsurin Park, Takamatsu City, Kagawa Prefecture.
Early Edo period.

*Garden of the Former Tachibana House, Yanagawa City, Fukuoka Prefecture.
Middle Edo period.*

THE APPEAL OF DRY LANDSCAPE GARDENS

▲ *Achi Shrine, Kurashiki City, Okayama Prefecture. Date uncertain.*

Mt. Shumisen composition, Upper Garden, Saiho-ji (Moss Temple), Kyoto. Nambokucho period.

▶ *Stone garden, Ryoan-ji, Kyoto. Muromachi period.*

Daisen-in, Daitoku-ji compound, Kyoto.
Muromachi period.

14

Main garden of Taizo-in, Myoshin-ji compound, Kyoto.
Muromachi period.

Shinnyo-in garden, Kyoto.
Momoyama period.

16

Manshu-in garden, Kyoto.
Early Edo period.

Tokai-an garden, Myoshin-ji compound, Kyoto.
Late Edo period.

II
Garden-Planning as an Art

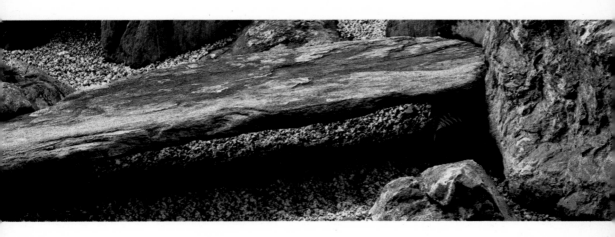

THE IMMUTABILITY OF STONES

Stone composition with "meditation stone" (right),
Saiho-ji (Moss Temple), Kyoto.
Muromachi period.

Lake and dry waterfall composition, Tenryu-ji, Kyoto. Nambokucho period.

Stone composition near the main building, Kinkaku-ji (Golden Pavilion), Kyoto.

Muromachi period.
Islet of Standing Stone, Kameishi-bo Temple, Fukuoka Prefecture.
Muromachi period.

General view of Joei-ji garden, Yamaguchi City, Yamaguchi Prefecture.
Muromachi period.

Tortoise Islet and trimmed shrubs, Iko-ji, Masuda City, Shimane Prefecture. Muromachi period.

Rocks in the garden of the Former Senshu-kaku Pavilion, Tokushima City, Tokushima Prefecture.
Momoyama period.

"Sixteen-disciples-of-the-Buddha" stone composition, Shuon-an, Kyoto Pre-fecture.
Early Edo period.

"Stone ship" at *Renge-ji, Kyoto.*
Early Edo period.

Stone composition of the Tsuki-no-Katsura Garden, Bofu City, Yamaguchi Prefecture.
Middle Edo period.

29

The Buddhist Paradise and
the Land of Eternal Youth and Immortality

▲ *Crane and Tortoise Garden at Konchi-in, Nanzen-ji compound, Kyoto.*
Early Edo period.

Garden in front of Hoö-do (Phoenix Hall), Byodo-in, Uji City, Kyoto Prefecture.
Middle Heian period.

Shumisen composition, Mampuku-ji, Masuda City, Shimane Prefecture. Muromachi period.

◀ *Pond-garden and pagoda, Joruri-ji, Kyoto Prefecture. Late Heian period.*

THE HARMONY OF GARDENS AND
BUILDINGS
34

View of garden from Inner Shoin,
Taga Taisha Shrine, Shiga Prefecture. Momoyama perioc

Trimmed shrubs and Main Hall, Jiko-in,
Yamato-Koriyama City, Nara Prefecture.
Early Edo period.

Pond-garden by pavilion, Hoshun-in, Daitoku-ji compound, Kyoto.
Early Edo period.

South Garden, Tofuku-ji, Kyoto.
Building reconstructed in 1890, garden remodeled in 1938.

37

PATHS TO THE TEAHOUSE

▲ *The Shonan-tei Teahouse and garden, Saiho-ji (Moss Temple), Kyoto. Nambokucho period.*

▶ *Path to the Sekka-tei Teahouse, Kinkaku-ji (Golden Pavilion), Kyoto. Muromachi period.*

Resting-place, Katsura Imperial Villa, Kyoto.
Early Edo period.

Path to the Kogetsu-tei Teahouse, Kanden-an, Matsue City, Shimane Prefecture.
Middle Edo period.

Path to the Fushin-an Teahouse, Omote Senke School, Kyoto.
Early Edo period. Rebuilt in 1913.

Path to the Yuin Teahouse, Ura Senke School, Kyoto.
Early Edo period.

View from the Bosen Tearoom, Koho-an, Daitoku-ji compound, Kyoto.
Middle Edo period.

Shogetsu-tei Teahouse, Sambo-in, Daigo-ji, Kyoto.
Momoyama period.

Miniature Scenery and Distant Scenery

▲ *View from the Upper Garden, Shugaku-in Imperial Villa, Kyoto. Early Edo period.*

▶ *Entsu-ji garden with Mt. Hiei in background, Kyoto. Early Edo period.*

Part of Sengan-en (Iso Park) with Mt. Sakurajima in background,
Kagoshima City, Kagoshima Prefecture.
Early Edo period.

View from Sekisui-in, Kozan-ji, Kyoto.
Late Edo period.

Miniature Ama-no-Hashidate ("Bridge of Heaven") viewed from the Shokin-tei Teahouse, Katsura Imperial Villa, Kyoto. Early Edo period.

Miniature Mt. Fuji and surroundings at Joju-en, Suizen-ji, Kumamoto City,
Kumamoto Prefecture.
Early Edo period.

Tsubo Niwa ("Jar Gardens")

Tsubo niwa *at Ninna-ji, Kyoto.*
Rebuilt in 1914 (originally Heian period

Tsubo niwa *Totekiko, Ryogen-in, Daitoku-ji compound, Kyoto.*
Muromachi period.

FLOWERING TREES AND COLORING LEAVES

Five-hundred-year-old "double-blossomed" cherry tree, Joshoko-ji,
Kyoto Prefecture.
Late Edo period.

Cherry trees and magnolias at Chikurin-in, Nara Prefecture.
Momoyama period.

Maple trees in the South Garden at Koto-in, Daitoku-ji compound, Kyoto.
Date of construction unknown.

*Old maple tree at Mantoku-ji, Obama City, Fukui Prefecture.
Early Edo period.*

Plum Orchard, Shozan, Kyoto.
Showa period.

Materials and the Sense of Beauty

THE RHYTHM OF TRIMMING

*Trimming at Raikyu-ji, Takahashi City, Okayama Prefecture.
Momoyama-Edo periods.*

Trimmed shrubs at Shoden-ji, Kyoto.
Early Edo period.

61

The Sound of Waterfalls and Streams

▲ *Oldest waterfall composition, Nakoso-no-Taki, Daikaku-ji, Kyoto. Date uncertain.*

▶ *Waterfall and pond-garden, Erin-ji, Enzan-shi, Yamanashi Prefect Kamakura-Nambokucho periods.*

Dry waterfall composition, Saimyo-ji, Shiga Prefecture.
Early Edo period.

Sengetsusen waterfall, Ginkaku-ji (Silver Pavilion), Kyoto.
Muromachi period.

Waterfall at Jakko-in, Kyoto.
Late Edo period.

▶ *Stream of Inner Garden, Kyoto Imperial Palace, Kyoto.*
Early Edo period.

Stream at Murin-an Villa, Kyoto.
Meiji period.

BRIDGES

▲ *Bridge with roofed resting-place, Eiho-ji, Tajimi City, Gifu Prefecture.*
Kamakura-Nambokucho periods.

Stone bridge in front of the Devotional Hall, Ginkaku-ji (Silver Pavilion), Kyoto.
Muromachi period.

Stone bridge with a wisteria arbor, South Garden,
Sento Imperial Palace, Kyoto.
Early Edo Period.

Wooden bridges in Genkyu-en, Hikone City, Shiga Prefecture.
Momoyama or early Edo period.

*Stone bridge and earthen bridge in Shukkei-en, Hiroshima City,
Hiroshima Prefecture.
Early Edo period.*

Stone bridge, Former Senshu-kaku Pavilion, Tokushima City,
Tokushima Prefecture.
Momoyama period.

STEPPING-STONES, PAVEMENTS, AND PATHS

▲ *"Stepping-stone steps" and the Kojo-kan Gate, Saiho-ji (Moss Temple), Kyoto.*
Nambokucho period.

75

Rear approach to Kozan-ji, Kyoto.
Late Edo period.

*Pavement of Shinju-an, Daitoku-ji compound, Kyoto.
Muromachi period.*

Pavement to the carriage approach, Katsura Imperial Villa, Kyoto.
Early Edo period.

Stepping-stones in the moss, Katsura Imperial Villa, Kyoto.
Early Edo period.

Path in Lower Garden, Shugaku-in Imperial Villa, Kyoto.
Early Edo period.

Stone step and mosaic of the Rin'un-tei Summer-house, Shugaku-in Imperial Villa, Kyoto.
Early Edo period.

Landing-place in Upper Garden, Shugaku-in Imperial Villa, Kyoto.
Early Edo period.

Pavement of the Ura Senke School, Kyoto.
Early Edo period.

Stepping-stones, Heian Shrine, Kyoto.
Taisho period.

83

SAND PATTERNS

▲ *Sand composition at Ginkaku-ji (Silver Pavilion), Kyoto.*
  Early Edo period.

▶ *South Garden of Daisen-in, Daitoku-ji compound, Kyoto.*
  Muromachi period.

Checkered pattern in front of Founder's Hall, Tofuku-ji, Kyoto.
Middle Edo period.

Sand composition, Bairin-ji, Kurume City, Fukuoka Prefecture.
Early Edo period.

Garden at Kishiwada Castle, Kishiwada City, Osaka Prefecture.
Showa period, 1952.

MOSS AND LAWNS

▲ *Moss-and-sand Garden of Funda-in, Tofuku-ji compound, Kyoto.*
Muromachi period, repaired in the Showa period.

89

Moss Garden at Heisen-ji, Katsuyama City, Fukui Prefecture.
End of Muromachi period.

*Stepping-stones, Shuko-en, Iizuka residence, Kashiwazaki City,
Niigata Prefecture.*
End of Edo period.

Moss Garden at Gio-ji, Kyoto.
Meiji period.

Moss design,
Sambo-in,
Daigo-ji,
Kyoto.
Taisho period.

Moss design, Rozan-ji, Kyoto.
Showa period.

Lawn in the dry landscape garden at Saiko-ji, Uwajima City, Ehime Prefecture.
Early Edo period.

Lawn in Rakusui-en, Jonan-gu Shrine, Kyoto.
Showa period.

Fence, Ginkaku-ji (Silver Pavilion), Kyoto.

FENCES AND GATES

Katsura fence, Katsura Imperial Villa, Kyoto.

Inner Gate of Omote Senke School, Kyoto.

Koetsu fence, Koetsu-ji, Kyoto.

Inner Gate of Keishun-in, Myoshin-ji compound, Kyoto.

Inner Gate, Villa of Kiyomizu Rokubei, Kyoto.

Water basin, Ura Senke School, Kyoto.

WATER BASINS

Water basin, Koho-an, Daitoku-ji compound, Kyoto.

Water basin, Ryoan-ji, Kyoto.

Water basin, Manshu-in, Kyoto.

Water basin, Kyu Ni-no-Maru Garden, Nagoya Castle,
Nagoya, Aichi Prefecture.

Washing-place, Katsura Imperial Villa, Kyoto.

STONE LANTERNS

▲ *Stone lanterns, Ryogen-in, Daitoku-ji compound, Kyoto*

▶ *Oribe-style stone lantern, Koho-an, Daitoku-ji compound, Kyoto*

OTHER ADORNMENTS

◄ Pine needles over the moss, Ura Senke School, Kyoto.

▲ Snow "umbrella," Kenroku-en, Kanazawa City, Ishikawa Prefecture.

Sozu, *Shisen-do, Kyoto*.

Japanese Gardens Revisited

ca. A.D. 552–645	Asuka period
645–794	Nara period
794–1185	Heian period
897–1185	Fujiwara period
1185–1336	Kamakura period
1336–1392	Nambokucho period
1392–1573	Muromachi period
1573–1615	Momoyama period
1615–1868	Edo (or Tokugawa) period
1868–1912	Meiji period
1912–1926	Taisho period
1926–	Showa period

NOTES:

1. The words *ji, in,* and *an* at the end of a name denote a temple. For example, Ryoan-ji could be translated as Ryoan Temple. Similarly, *en* denotes a garden. Thus, Sengan-en means Sengan Garden.
2. The numbers in brackets refer to pages in *Invitation to Japanese Gardens* (by the same authors)—[I, 54] thus indicating page fifty-four of that book.
3. The temples referred to in the text are in Kyoto unless otherwise stated.

1. *Hirosawa Pond.*   2. *East Garden, Toji-in.*

A Brief History of Japanese Gardens

The Natural Beauty of Pond-Gardens

According to *The Chronicles of Japan* (*Nihon Shoki*), the first Japanese pond-gardens were constructed at the end of the sixth century. Although the location of these original gardens is not known, it can be said that the now-classic pond or lake was established as a feature of Japanese gardens more than a thousand years ago.

Osawa Pond (p. 2) was first constructed by Emperor Saga in the ninth century as part of the garden of an imperial villa. As a pond-garden for boating (*chisen-shuyu-shiki*), it is typ cal of the period. Hirosawa Pond lies not far to the east of Osawa Pond and is part of the same garden complex. Time must have changed the ponds and their surroundings considerably, but from what remains one can easily imagine the grand scale of the original construction. The beauty of the Northern Sagano district owes much to these ponds.

On the left as one enters the precincts of Ryoan-ji lies Kyoyo-chi Pond (p. 3), which was constructed about 1180 as part of the garden of the villa of the Tokudaiji family. Unfortunately, this pond is all too often ignored by visitors to the temple, who hurry by to look at the well-known stone garden. Though now somewhat forlorn, it still reflects with its many islets the style of the Heian period.

The Zen priest Muso (1275–1351) is the greatest figure in the history of Japanese garden planning. His work demonstrates the

Fig. 1

3. *Yogoseki stone, Saiho-ji (Moss Temple).* 4. *Ginkaku-ji (Silver Pavilion).*

rigorous discipline of the Zen spirit as well as the graceful taste of the Heian court, as typified in the *zazen-ishi* ("Zen meditation stone") and in the overhanging cherry tree, both of which always find a place in his gardens. Of the many extant gardens attributed to Muso, those at Saiho-ji and Tenryu-ji are the finest.

Fig. 2   The East Garden at Toji-in is believed, though with less certainty, to have been constructed by him in 1339 (see also [I, 54]).

Ogon-chi Pond at Saiho-ji (Moss Temple) (p. 4) was possibily built around 1339 when Muso was appointed superior of the temple. The pond has the shape of the Chinese character for "heart." The tree trunks, the wooden bridges, the stones and rocks are all covered with moss. There is no feeling of artificiality. In the Lower Garden, of which the pond is a part, there is

Fig. 3   the *yogoseki* stone regarded as the guardian stone of the temple. The ponds at both Saiho-ji and Tenryu-ji are of the type called *kaiyu-shiki* (pond-gardens for strolling around). This type was the creation of Muso (see p. 21, Tenryu-ji).

Rokuon-ji, or Kinkaku-ji (Golden Pavilion) (p. 5), was constructed by the third Ashikaga shogun, Yoshimitsu, in 1397. The pavilion itself, being a recent reconstruction, has little historical or cultural significance, but the garden is a good example of the early Muromachi period. The islets in the pond symbolize the Buddhist paradise.

Fig. 4   Jisho-ji, or Ginkaku-ji (Silver Pavilion), was constructed by the eighth Ashikaga shogun, Yoshimasa. Kinkaku-ji and Ginkaku-ji were originally built in imitation of the Moss Temple,

*The numbers in brackets refer to pages in *Invitation to Japanese Gardens*, by the same authors.

116

5. *Kokei Garden, Nishi Hongan-ji.* 6. *Landing-place in front of the Shoiken Teahouse, Katsura Imperial Villa.*

which Yoshimitsu and Yoshimasa admired, but the resemblance survives on a small scale only in the Silver Pavilion.

At the end of the sixteenth century commenced the military governance of Japan by the Tokugawa family, and with it the construction of castles. The Kokei Garden, a miniature reproduction of the Kokei (Hugi) Garden in China, was first laid out in Fushimi Castle but later transferred to its present site at Nishi *Fig. 5* Hongan-ji. It reflects the grand style of the Momoyama period and Toyotomi Hideyoshi, conveying some idea of the castle garden of those days.

The construction of Katsura Imperial Villa was begun around 1620 by Prince Toshihito and completed more than forty years later by his son, Prince Toshitada. The refined taste of father and son is responsible for the exquisite harmony of the buildings and of the garden surrounding them (p. 6). Even the smallest corner is arranged with the greatest circumspection, and an artificial beauty seems to have superseded a natural one. This garden is the finest example of a pond-garden for strolling and boating, and its fusion of practicality and beauty is unsurpassed.

The tea ceremony (*cha-no-yu*) began in the Muromachi period and was brought to an accomplished form by the tea-master Sen-no-Rikyu during the Momoyama period. It had considerable influence on the construction of teahouses and paths leading to them. The ideal of a path to the teahouse was, in the main, simplicity and quiet, though elegant refinements were added later. This combination is best illustrated in the teahouses and their *Fig. 6* gardens beside the lake at Katsura Imperial Villa.

7. *Inner Garden, Kyoto Imperial Palace.*　　　　　　　　　8. *Pond-garden, Shoren-in.*

Nijo Castle was completed in 1605, and the Ni-no-Maru Garden (p. 7) seems to have been laid out at about the same time. The impressive arrangement of rocks and stones adds considerably to the overall grandeur of the garden, which is regarded as a masterpiece of the castle garden style.

In the garden at Joju-in (Abbot's Hall of Kiyomizu-dera) (p. 8), the islets, trees, and rocks are neatly arranged, and the exact placing of the stone lantern adds depth to this modest garden. The rather unusual *eboshi-iwa* (rock in the shape of the headgear of a court nobleman), on the right, is effective. This is one of the finest examples of the seventeenth-century pond-garden.

Fig. 7　　The Inner Garden at Kyoto Imperial Palace and the pond-
Fig. 8　garden at Shoren-in were also laid out in about the same period.

With the establishment of the feudal system, many *daimyo* (feudal lords) gained economic power and competed with one another in constructing large gardens on their estates. Techniques for the construction of pond-gardens for strolling, pond-gardens for boating, incorporated scenery, and miniature reproductions of famous sights were utilized. These attempts to combine various arts and skills of garden-planning only resulted in the loss of earlier boldness and its replacement by a feminine neatness. After repair and some remodeling, many of these *daimyo* gardens were turned into public parks after the end of the
Fig. 9　Tokugawa period. The Genkyu-en in Hikone, Shiga Prefecture, is one example.

The Ritsurin Park in Takamatsu, Ehime Prefecture (p. 9), has a total area of 700,000 square meters and is divided into North and South gardens. The North Garden is now a western-

118

9. *Genkyu-en.*   10. *Garden of the Nakai residence, near Nanzen-ji.*

style garden, following its rearrangement during the Meiji period. The South Garden has a lake, islets, rock compositions, stepping-stones, all in refined taste. They are the result of more than seventy years' attention by its wealthy original owners, the Matsudaira clan. The Kikugetsu-tei Teahouse is shown in the first volume [I, 96].

The garden at the Former Tachibana House in Yanagawa, Fukuoka Prefecture (p. 10), is another example of a garden attached to a daimyo mansion. It is a miniature reproduction of Matsushima, considered one of the three finest sights of Japan, and the pine trees are more than two hundred years old. The garden is famous for the many wild duck that visit it in winter.

The quality of gardens after the middle of the Edo period gradually deteriorated until the Meiji Restoration in 1868, when, with the opening of Japan, the influence of Western civilization began to be strongly felt in every sphere of culture. The Westernization of the garden was also attempted, but with little success. In the 1900's men of wealth built villas in the Higashiyama district near Nanzen-ji in Kyoto. Most of them took advantage of the rich water supply of nearby streams and had ponds with streams and waterfalls. Mt. Higashiyama served as a background to these gardens.

This type of garden is called the "naturalistic garden," and specialists tend to ignore it. But every garden has some natural characteristics, and these gardens, faithfully reproducing nature, have their own *raison d'être*. At least they gave a refreshing stimulus in an otherwise stagnant period of garden history. The

Fig. 10   garden at the Nakai House is an example of this type.

11. *Outer Shrine of Omiwa Shrine.*

The Appeal of Dry Landscape Gardens

A garden which represents nature in an abstract and symbolic way without using water is called a dry landscape garden (*kare-sansui*). Stones represent mountains, valleys, and waterfalls, and sand represents oceans, rivers, streams, and ponds. The intention is to portray the inner meaning rather than the external appearance. Thus this unique method enables us to grasp the intrinsic meaning of nature, which might otherwise lie hidden from us.

Ancient Japanese worshipped mountains as the incarnation *Fig. 11* of gods. Omiwa Shrine in Nara Prefecture is a well-known example of this type of shrine, where the inner shrine is the mountain itself. There are also shrines where huge rocks are placed at the top of the mountain so that gods may descend onto them. It could be said that the immutable and eternal quality of stone has inspired the deification. Some garden historians consider these to be the archetype of the dry landscape garden. They are in fact different from the stone compositions in landscape gardens, but the arrangement of those huge rocks must have been accomplished with a simple and naïve aesthetic consciousness towards formative art. So it is not unreasonable to see some analogy with the stone compositions of the dry landscape garden which developed later.

The dry garden in its early form, explained, for example, in the *Book of Garden-Planning (Sakuteiki)*, written in the Kamakura period, was a dry part of the pond-garden in which an arrangement of standing stones formed an artificial hill. In the garden *Fig. 12* at Motsu-ji, Hiraizumi, Iwate Prefecture, there is a composition

12. *Motsu-ji garden.* 13. *Dry waterfall composition, Saiho-ji (Moss Temple).*

of standing stones at the tip of a peninsula that reminds one of this earlier form of dry garden.

Later on, the dry part of the garden became independent and developed along its own path. We now call this the dry landscape garden. From the mid-fifteenth century, this type was laid out chiefly in Zen temples. The appearance of the dry landscape garden marks a new era in the history of the Japanese garden, and the best of the kind have more intensity and attractiveness as formative art than the pond-garden.

Gardens are usually created to bring pleasure to our daily lives. Gardens in Zen temples, however, try to represent the Zen spirit of total denial, and when the dry landscape garden was most closely joined with the Zen spirit, it became the other main current of the Japanese garden.

The Achi Shrine, in Kurashiki, Okayama Prefecture (p. 11), is another example of what is thought to be the archetype of the dry landscape garden.

Fig. 13 The Upper Garden at Saiho-ji (Moss Temple) has three stone compositions: the one shown on page twelve symbolizes Mt. Shumisen, the Buddhist paradise; the one shown here represents a dry waterfall [I, 66]; and the third on page twenty is a "meditation stone." The Mt. Shumisen composition is possibly one of the earliest examples of a dry landscape garden which has become separated from a pond-garden. The naturalness owes much to the skill of the great Zen priest Muso. The waterfall composition symbolizes three levels of a mountain fall. It is so magnificent that one almost feels that real water is flowing rapidly among the stones.

14. *Ryoan-ji garden.*

Fig. 14   The stone garden at Ryoan-ji (p. 13) is supposed to have been laid out about 1499, but the planner is not known. The garden is an oblong strip of land of about 330 square meters, and the materials of the composition are only white sand and fifteen stones arranged in the series 5–2–3–2–3 (from east to west), in what is called the "seven-five-three" style. From whatever location in the Abbot's Hall the stones are viewed, one is always hidden behind the others and only fourteen can be seen. These stones are generally believed to represent islands in an ocean, but the composition is called Tora-no-Ko Watashi (Tiger Cubs Crossing a Stretch of Water). Whatever the original intention may have been, it need not trouble the observer. Here he will find peace and can interpret the garden as he wishes. This garden is certainly the acme of simplicity and rigor combined with high refinement, and seems always to have in reserve new attractions to be discovered by the viewer.

Daisen-in, within the Daitoku-ji compound, has two gardens: the front garden of the Abbot's Hall and the northeast garden (p. 14). The latter was built in 1513, and was placed in the abbot's living quarters so that he might observe it and meditate upon it at any time. Though it is only one hundred square meters in area, it is famous for its power to conjure up the illusion of space. Water runs from the waterfall, represented by the large rocks at the back, out into a valley, and then, spreading further, meets the sea, which washes around islands and ships [I, 48]. Reminiscent of Chinese landscapes sketched in black and white, it is comparable with the Ryoan-ji garden as one of the finest examples of the dry landscape garden.

15. *Ryogen-in garden.*   16. *Juko-in garden.*

The main garden of Taizo-in (p. 15), Myoshin-ji compound, is believed to be the work of the great painter Kano Motonobu. It shows clearly the colorful technique of the Kano school [I, 55].

Fig. 15   The garden at Ryogen-in, Daitoku-ji compound, is of the same period. It is a "three-in-one" stone composition (*sanzon ishi-gumi*), which literally means a stone composition in the form of Buddha standing between two accompanying saints (see [I, 51] and Glossary "*sanzon iwagumi*").

The garden at Shinnyo-in of the Nichiren sect (p. 16) is attributed to Oda Nobunaga. It is a miniature reproduction of a natural landscape, and its focal point is the dry stream of scale-shaped grey-colored pebbles neatly spread over the river bed. This elaborate and rare technique is effective here. The garden was transferred to the present site and reconstructed with the original materials during the Second World War.

Fig. 16   The Juko-in garden, Daitoku-ji compound, is also of the Momoyama period.

The dry landscape garden changed with the passage of time from symbolic to naturalistic representation. Technical skills and structures became variegated by the use of superb stone compositions, trimmed hedges, and foreign trees such as cycad. Initially, only Zen priests and artisans planned this type of garden, but at the end of the sixteenth century there arose a tendency to allow samurai and then people of any rank to do so. The best among them was Kobori Enshu, an official who dealt with affairs concerning the Imperial Household and the Tokugawa shogunate while at the same time showing his versatility in garden-planning, tea ceremony, and other arts.

17. *Manshu-in.*

Fig. 17   The construction of the garden at Manshu-in (p. 17) w
carried out by Kobori Enshu's followers under the direction
Priest-Prince Ryosho. The garden is in front of the well-bui
shoin. In the southeast corner a dry waterfall is boldly repr
sented by a huge upright rock. The big stone bridge in front
it also reflects the taste of the period. The dry stream flows int
an expanse of white sand symbolizing waves lapping aroun
islands of foliage. This garden with its aristocratic atmospher
is notable for innovations to the traditional style and structur
of the dry garden.

As the dry garden developed structurally and technically i
various directions, the essential skill of composing stones de
clined drastically. This is partly because it had lost its inne
contact with the Zen spirit. Gradually the creation of dry gar
dens became rare, but there were some attempts to resist thi
decline.

The garden at Tokai-an (p. 18) is one of them. It was buil
in 1874 in a very small area of sixteen square meters, with whit
sand and seven stones. The exquisite simplicity of this garde
seems to be an expression of the Zen doctrine of total denial

GARDEN-PLANNING AS AN ART

The Immutability of Stones

In the pond-garden, in spite of the extensive use of stones,
water is the main constituent. In the dry landscape garden, however, stones are dominant and form the framework of the whole

18. *Tenryu-ji garden.*

structure. They have an eternal sculptural beauty and a look of antiquity. With the appearance of dry gardens, the handling of stones, techniques, and skills of stone composition showed a remarkable improvement and progress.

The Zen priest Muso is said to have done his Zen training on the "meditation stone" in the Upper Garden at Saiho-ji (p. 20). The massive quality of the stone is overwhelming, and the composition is grandeur itself.

Fig. 18   The garden at Tenryu-ji (p. 21) is considered to be a late work of Muso. Though the garden is also intended for strolling, the emphasis is on viewing it from the Abbot's Hall. A dry waterfall in the center of the hill has a rather elaborate composition in two levels with biggish rocks, and the invisible water rushes down from the deep recesses of the hill. The stone bridge, made of three natural flat stones, two of which are arranged in a straight line with the third put a little to one side (more clearly seen in [I, 60]), is said to be the oldest of the kind placed in front of the waterfall. To the right in the photograph on page twenty-one is seen an islet made of a pin-pointed stone and seven other rocks; the tip of a peninsula is seen in the foreground. The existence of the peninsula which protrudes far into the lake is effectively emphasized by the stone arrangement of the lake bank. The garden is, so to speak, a blending of the elegant manner of Yamato-e genre painting and the Zen-style rigidity of Chinese landscape painting. The harmony is unique and perfect. The elegant manner of the Yamato-e can be said to be a continuous line from the pond-garden at the Moss Temple through that at Tenryu-ji to that at the Golden Pavilion.

19. *Yodomari-ishi composition, Saiho-ji (Moss Temple).*   20. *Ama-no-Hashidate ("Bridge of Heaven") by Sessh*

The *yodomari-ishi* composition at Kinkaku-ji (Golden Pa
vilion) (p. 22) is achieved by four stones placed in a line in th
pond beside the pavilion, symbolizing ships at anchor, ready t
set out to seek the treasures of paradise, and so the stones ar
close to the building.

Fig. 19   The same kind of arrangement is to be found in the pond a
the Moss Temple, where the stones are placed at exquisite in
tervals in two lines. It is also found in the pond at Tenryu-ji.

Fig. 20   Sesshu (1420–1506), one of the greatest Japanese masters o
Chinese-style landscape painting, was also a priest. His painting
still survive in large numbers, but very little is known abou
his life. In spite of no definite evidence of his attempts at garden
planning, there are several temple gardens attributed to him

The garden at Kameishibo in Fukuoka Prefecture (p. 23)
built around 1470, is one of them. It is a pond-garden for view
ing from the buildings of the temple, which were destroyed
long ago. It has a dry waterfall composition on the hillside be
yond the pond, and the bank composition and the stone islets
emphasize the well-preserved immutable quality of stones.

The garden at Joei-ji in Yamaguchi City is another fine example, believed to have been laid out by Sesshu around 1478.
This is the largest and possibly the best among those attributed
to him. The ground of 2,640 square meters is divided into the
Inner and Outer gardens. The Inner Garden (p. 24) has a pond
Fig. 21   in the center, several islets, a waterfall composition at the
northern part with what is generally called the "sixteen-disciples-of-the-Buddha" stone composition and a "meditation
stone" nearby. In the front garden of the Main Hall, there are

21. *Waterfall composition, Joei-ji.*

many stones scattered on the lawn and also among the numerous small trimmed shrubs. The stones, large and small, seemingly placed at random, are actually laid with great care and originality. The stone in the shape of Mt. Fuji symbolizes Japan, while other stones symbolize the mountains of China. Thus the marvelous arrangement of the garden can be regarded as a painting or a poem worthy of a master. Sesshu is said to have admired Muso and to have been indirectly influenced by him. It is not difficult for us to find here some resemblance to the gardens built by Muso.

The garden at Iko-ji, Masuda City, Shimane Prefecture (p. 25), is also attributed to Sesshu. He is believed to have been the fifth abbot of the temple. The site of 990 square meters is divided into two levels. The pond in the shape of a half-moon has an islet connected to the land by a stone bridge, and there are trimmed hedges on the hill beyond. The general view not only resembles the landscape paintings of Sesshu, but also reveals a similarity to Muso's techniques of garden-planning in the addition of an overhanging cherry tree (not shown in the photograph). The main building was destroyed in the middle of the Edo period but, together with the garden, was repaired soon after. The trimmed hedge is supposed to have been added at that time.

The Momoyama period garden at the Former Senshu-kaku

22. *Stone composition in Tsuki-no-Katsura Garden.*

Pavilion in Tokushima Castle (p. 26) is the forerunner of the so-called daimyo gardens built in the early Edo period. It has both a pond-garden for strolling and a dry garden. The pond contains seawater and is full of the blue stones which are found in this district. The strange and sometimes grotesque shapes and colors of these stones is one of the characteristics of this garden. The dry garden has a huge bridge of natural blue-stone ten meters long (p. 74).

The East Garden at Shuon-an, in Kyoto Prefecture (p. 27), has a "sixteen-disciples-of-the-Buddha" stone composition, suggesting that those disciples remain in this world eternally to ensure the correct teaching of Buddhism. Sixteen stones are placed as if casually along the mud wall. The flowing impression of this composition gives the viewer a feeling of ease after the rigorousness of the Zen spirit embodied in the North Garden, a part of which is seen in the above left corner of the photograph [cf. I, 75].

The pond-garden at Renge-ji (p. 28), which receives water from the nearby Takano River, has a natural stone in the shape of a ship setting out in search of treasure.

Fig. 22   The Tsuki-no-Katsura Garden in Bofu City, Yamaguchi Prefecture (p. 29), is a dry flat garden of eighty square meters, built in 1712. It may have been suggested by the sand, stones, and mud-walls of Ryoan-ji in Kyoto, but the impression is quite different. The stone composition on the sand is surprisingly original. The *tsuki-no-katsura* is a great laurel tree that in Chinese legend is believed to exist on the moon.

The Buddhist Paradise and the Land of Eternal Youth and Immortality

From the very beginning, Japanese gardens have been open to the influences of foreign thought, among the most prominent being those of Buddhism and Taoism, which entered Japan around the middle of the sixth century. The most tangible result of their influence was the emergence of the concepts of the Buddhist paradise (*Jodo*) and the Heavenly Island where, according to Chinese Taoism, grow miraculous herbs that give eternal youth and immortality.

Some readers may insist that the religious background to Japanese gardens is so complex and difficult that it is not essential to their appreciation. But since religious styles and manners have been utilized in past garden-planning, and the tradition has been the main current, it is impossible to ignore the religious elements. Yet here lies another problem. The religious elements are so complex that even connoisseurs may disagree whether one garden should be interpreted in the traditions of Buddhism or of Taoism. For the average viewer it would seem best to have a general idea of the religious background, and then to judge for himself.

The garden at Konchi-in, Nanzen-ji compound (p. 30), is a splendid achievement of Kobori Enshu, and is generally considered representative of the "crane and tortoise" style, that is, a garden having the two symbolic islets, the "crane" and the "tortoise." They are symbols of long life, as is seen in the old saying: "A crane lives a thousand and a tortoise ten thousand years." In the Chinese conception of paradise, however, the crane represents the male and the tortoise the female; together they represent the harmony of the male and female principles, that is, the prosperity of the offspring. The photograph shows the crane islet on the left, and a large flat stone called the prayer stone to the right. In the background is seen the paradise represented by trimmed shrubs.

Fig. 23   There are many pond-gardens and dry gardens that represent this crane and tortoise motif. The garden at Sambo-in is one of them.

23. *Sambo-in garden.* 24. *Nine images of Amida, Joruri-ji.*

The garden of Hoö-do (Phoenix Hall), the Amida Hall of Byodo-in (p. 31), was built by Fujiwara Yorimichi in 1053. After repairs, it made a welcome and spectacular reappearance in March 1957. From it we can glimpse the paradisaic world which the nobles of those days wished to see in their dreams.

Fig. 24 The garden at Joruri-ji in Kyoto Prefecture (p. 32) was built in 1150. Beyond the pond with its many water lilies lie the Main Hall which enshrines nine images of Amida and a beautiful three-story pagoda. Many repairs have altered the original form, but when the nine golden images of Amida are reflected on the water of the pond, it really makes one feel that such must be the pond of paradise.

The garden at Mampuku-ji, Masuda City, Shimane Prefecture, is attributed to Sesshu. It is a pond-garden for strolling, and the hill beyond the pond represents Mt. Shumisen, which is in Buddhism the central mountain of the world, and which symbolizes the Land of Eternal Happiness. The stone composition arranged on the hillside with the "Shumisen stone" on top is a rarity of its kind (p. 33).

The Harmony of Gardens and Buildings

A garden and a building, or buildings, in combination are said to form an indivisible unit. In general, the garden is likely to be considered subordinate to the building, but this was not necessarily the case in ancient times. At that time, due partially to the immaturity of the art of building, the outdoor area was frequently preferred to the indoor. The South Garden of the

25. *South Garden of the Shishinden (Ceremonial Hall), Kyoto Imperial Palace.*

26. *View of the garden with the Gepparo Teahouse in the distance, Katsura Imperial Villa.*

Fig. 25   Shishinden (Ceremonial Hall) in the Kyoto Imperial Palace is a noteworthy instance in which the garden was used only for important ceremonies, and was therefore more important than the Hall itself. As time passed, everything came to be performed indoors, and the garden became an ornament whose beauty was enhanced if the buildings were in harmony with it.

Fig. 26   Katsura Imperial Villa is a superb example of the achievement of such harmony.

Taga Taisha is the oldest shrine in Shiga Prefecture. The building is of recent construction, but the pond-garden (p. 34) was built in the Momoyama period. In the far corner of the garden is an overhanging cherry tree, which, when in full blossom, adds to the antique charm of the garden. The portraits on the wall above are of the "thirty-six major poets" of Japan.

The garden of Jiko-in, Yamato-Koriyama City, Nara Prefecture (p. 35), is famous for its big trimmed trees. The main building, which reminds us of the thatched dwelling of a wealthy farmer, is well matched with the trimmed shrubs surrounding it.

Both the garden and the pavilion of Hoshun-in, Daitoku-ji compound (p. 36), are generally considered to have been built by Kobori Enshu under the orders of Maeda Toshiie. The Donko-kaku Pavilion, regarded as one of the five finest pavilions in Kyoto, is the focal point of the garden. The garden is included in a book called *Miyako Rinsen Meisho-zue* (Pictures of Famous Scenic Gardens in Kyoto), compiled in the Edo period, and, except that the bridge is depicted not as a stone bridge but

131

as a wooden one, it appears in that book almost as it does today (cf. [I, 142]).

The South Garden of the Abbot's Hall, Tofuku-ji compound (p. 37), was laid out by Shigemori Mirei in 1938. The stone composition here symbolizes the four Elysian islands. Five hills to the right (not shown here) symbolize the headquarters of the five major sects of Buddhism. The building, the gate, and the wall are an integral part of the garden.

Paths to the Teahouse

The tea ceremony (cha-no-yu) was brought to perfection by Sen-no-Rikyu in the middle of the sixteenth century. The place where tea is taken is called a chashitsu, or the tearoom proper, and the path to the teahouse that includes the tearoom is called a roji (path) or chatei (teahouse garden). Rikyu considered the orthodox path to be like an untrodden way to a hut. This "hut" is the "hut-style" teahouse, the ideal of which is to enjoy the tea of the common people. In contrast, Furuta Oribe, from a samurai family, propagated the tea ceremony among the upper class and built teahouses and paths in shoin style. Kobori Enshu, who followed him, also developed the aristocratic tearoom and teahouse.

Thus a new type of garden was created, and it was introduced into both pond-gardens and dry gardens. It has had a great influence over the later development of Japanese gardens.

The teahouse garden consists of a path from the gate to the teahouse, with the addition of inner gate, assembly annex, privy, water basin, and stone lantern, placed in appropriate relationship. The path being the way to the teahouse, practicality counts before beauty to the eye; the ideal of a path may be said to lie in a happy combination of practicality and beauty. After grasping the spirit of the tea ceremony, when one follows the stepping-stones of the path to the teahouse it is easy to appreciate this subtle world.

Fig. 27
Fig. 28

No teahouse built in the age of Rikyu has survived in a complete form, but the Tai-an Teahouse at the Myoki-an Zen Hermitage, Oyamazaki, Kyoto Prefecture, and the Shigure-tei and Karakasa-tei teahouses at Kodai-ji, Kyoto, are noted in connection with Rikyu.

The Shonan-tei Teahouse at Saiho-ji (p. 38) was reconstructed about 350 years ago by Shoan, the second son of Sen-no-Rikyu,

27. *Path to the Tai-an Teahouse, Myoki-an.*   28. *Shigure-tei and Karakasa-tei teahouses, Kodai-ji.*

after the original built by Muso. The structure of the teahouse, especially the verandah with its simple railings, the pillars of natural timber, and the ceiling daubed with plaster, is unusual for a teahouse. In the front garden are arranged stepping-stones among the moss, and a small stone basin at the foot of a tree, each seeming to be set in its ideal position.

The stepping-stones leading to the front of the Sekka-tei Teahouse at Kinkaku-ji (p. 39) are of various shapes. To the right, behind the fence, one can see a stone lantern and a very famous water basin of natural stone in the shape of Mt. Fuji, which was prized by Yoshimasa, the founder of the Golden Pavilion. Close to the large stone lantern (to the left in the photograph) there is a stone seat for a high personage, which was moved from the site of the Muromachi shogunate. The teahouse was originally built by Kanamori Sowa, but the present one is a 1875 reconstruction.

The resting-place at the Katsura Imperial Villa (p. 40) was used as an assembly annex for participants in the tea ceremony at the Shokin-tei Teahouse. It has a thatched hip-roof supported by pillars of natural wood and is open on all sides. The pavement in front is composed of both hewn and natural stones. A square water basin and a lantern are seen to the left.

Fig. 29 At the top of a hill, at the back of the Shokin-tei Teahouse, stands a square arbor called Manji-tei. It was used as a resting-place in the intervals of the tea ceremony held in Shokin-tei. There are four seats, each varying in shape and size, placed in swastika fashion so that no two people may sit face to face. It is a very simple but unique contrivance.

29. *Manji-tei, Katsura Imperial Villa.*

Kanden-an in Matsue City, Shimane Prefecture, is a teahouse built in the villa of a principal retainer of the Matsudaira clan, under the direction of Matsudaira Fumai in 1792. The photograph (p. 41) shows the path to the Kogetsu-tei Teahouse, built by Hyoan, Fumai's younger brother. The thick bamboo stems attached to the stone pavements reveal the unique and refined taste of the designer.

There are three Senke schools of tea, all founded by the descendants of Sen-no-Rikyu, the principal masters of the tea ceremony: they are the Omote Senke, the Ura Senke, and the Musshanokoji Senke. Fushin-an, Konnichi-an, and Kankyu-an are, respectively, the three representative teahouses of these schools, and the names of the teahouses are used to designate their schools.

The original Fushin-an, built by Rikyu in front of the gate of Daitoku-ji, was destroyed at about the time of his death. It was restored by Shoan, Rikyu's son, but was subsequently leveled by fire several times. The present teahouse (p. 42) is a 1913 reconstruction. The structure and the site of the teahouse as well as the path have undergone many changes, but the present building and the path preserve the orthodox tradition of the hut style in the manner of Rikyu. The Inner Gate (*nakakuguri*) [I, 44], on the path between the assembly annex and the Zangetsu-tei Teahouse, is well known.

The Yu-in (p. 43) is as important a teahouse in the Ura Senke School as the Konnichi-an. It is said that Sotan, grandson of Rikyu, built Yu-in in order to use it after retirement, having given Konnichi-an to his son Shoshitsu. Sotan must have used

30. *Path to Kankyu-an Teahouse, Mushanokoji Senke School.*

31. *Yushin Teahouse, Ura Senke School.*

stones that were readily available: the stepping-stones before the entrance remind one of a handful of beans thrown here and there; hence they are sometimes called Stepping-Stones in Disorder, sometimes Stones Scattered Like Beans.

Fig. 30 The path to the Kankyu-an Teahouse is well known as being representative of the Mushanokoji Senke School.

Fig. 31 In order to catch up with the contemporary change in taste and customs, the Ura Senke School built a new tearoom, Yushin, so that overseas visitors might take part in the tea ceremony with some degree of comfort. The old and the new teahouses go together in harmony here.

The illustration on page forty-four is the famous view from the Bosen Tearoom of Koho-an, the Daitoku-ji compound, which attempts to give the effect of looking out from inside a ship. It was originally built in 1612 by Kobori Enshu as his family temple and place of retirement in the Ryuko-in compound at Daitoku-ji. It was moved to its present site thirty-one years later. Although it was destroyed by fire in 1793, the skill of the great master is still preserved through the faithful restoration by Matsudaira Fumai. The name of the Bosen Tearoom ("Forget the Net") refers to the fact that once a fish has been caught one no longer concerns oneself with the net, suggesting the life that rises above mere material gain and earthly power. Kobori Enshu himself, having retired from government affairs, must have wished to lead such a life.

Under the Shogetsu-tei Teahouse in the Sambo-in compound (p. 45) runs the water of the lake; a support of the teahouse

32. *Yoshino-mado window, Shogetsu-tei Teahouse, Sambo-in.*

Fig. 32

stands in mid-stream. The water basin is also placed in the stream. The wooden bridge in the front adds to the general atmosphere of neatness, lightness, and delicacy. There is a round window (*yoshino-mado*) in the tearoom, through which participants in the tea ceremony may enjoy the view.

Miniature Scenery and Distant Scenery

The technique of incorporating distant scenery such as mountains, rivers, fields, and villages into the garden is called *shakkei*. It has the effect of emphasizing the depth of the garden and of adding charm. Undesirable objects in the background are concealed by the planting of trees within the garden, thereby fusing garden and background into a harmonious picture. But we must not forget in viewing such a garden that the garden itself is more important than the borrowed scenery, which, in some cases, tends to attract the viewer more.

The origin of this technique is unknown, but Osawa Pond (p. 2) and the view of the garden from the Hoö-do Hall of Byodo-in (p. 31) are possibly the earliest examples of the unintentional use of background scenery. One of the earliest examples of intentional incorporation is probably the garden at

Fig. 33

Tenryu-ji with Arashiyama in the background. This garden dates

33. *Tenryu-ji garden with Mt. Arashiyama in back-ground.*

from around 1340, though the word *shakkei* had not been coined at that time.

The background scenery can alter in time; for example, urban areas may replace fields. The borrowing of Mt. Hiei has now been completely lost in the East Garden of the Abbot's Hall at Daitoku-ji, and in the Seven-Five-Three Garden at Shinju-an [I, 46]. Weather also alters the borrowing: compare the two photographs of the Entsu-ji garden ([I, 34] and p. 47).

Although the Shugaku-in Imperial Villa was dealt with in *Invitation to Japanese Gardens* [I, 136–38], let me again touch briefly upon the Upper Garden (pp. 46–47), which utilizes the *shakkei* technique on possibly the grandest scale. It is proof of consummate skill fit only for an emperor. It is easily imaginable that Emperor Gomizunoö, who directed the construction of the villa, was fascinated by the grand view and thought of incoporating the scenery beyond the garden to make it the highlight of the whole villa. Bruno Taut, the German architect, praised its grandeur as the expression of an early Japanese cosmopolitanism.

The garden at Entsu-ji (p. 47) is also a typical *shakkei* garden. It is a wide rectangular dry garden of green moss with groups of stones and bushes. Far in the distance beyond the hedge is seen the beautiful shape of Mt. Hiei between the trees, like a drawing on a folding screen (*byobu*), the trees giving the effect of the folding line. When it was first made in 1678, however, the trees could not have existed, because they are far less than three hundred years old. Originally, the entire shape of Mt. Hiei must have been visible. No matter whether those trees were planted in later years or grew out from seed, the present effect is of interest and appealing to the eye.

Sengan-en or Iso Park, Kagoshima City (p. 48), was originally built as part of a villa by Shimazu Mitsuhisa of the Kagoshima clan, and is now open to the public as Iso Park. The photograph shows a part of the park, with an impressive view of Mt. Sakurajima behind. The mountain, a famous volcano with a unique shape, alters its color according to the time of the day and the weather.

The view from Sekisui-en at Kozan-ji (p. 49) is not exactly a *shakkei*, nor is it intended to borrow the scenery around it. The simple but elegant building, destroyed by a fire in 1881 and reconstructed at the present site in 1889, is placed in the midst of beautiful surroundings to produce a superb example of union between a building and nature.

The device of reproducing famous sights, scenery, or scenic beauty on a smaller scale to form a part or the center of a garden is called *shukukei* or *shukkei* (miniature scenery). Among the most popular models have been Lushan, Si-hu (West Lake), the Eight Scenic Views around Tungting Lake in China, Mt. Fuji, the Scenic Trio of Japan, and, after the Chinese Eight Views, the Eight Scenic Views around Lake Biwa. They are reproduced more or less realistically, but when (as in the case of Lushan, for example), the model is unknown to most Japanese, the tendency can be said to be closer to symbolical representation. The symbolic touch predominates especially when the model is imaginary, such as the sacred site of the Buddhist world or the ideal world reproduced in many dry landscapes of Zen temples.

The view from the Shokin-tei Teahouse in Katsura Imperial Villa (p. 50) shows the two islets connected by stone bridges with the land, representing in miniature Ama-no-Hashidate, "Bridge of Heaven," upon which, according to Japanese mythology, the gods Izanagi and Izanami stood while they created Japan. This is one of the most beautiful sights of the garden, and the simplification rather than realistic representation has been successful in enhancing its beauty.

Joju-en at Suizen-ji, Kumamoto City (p. 51), is a daimyo garden famous for its miniature scenery. The photograph shows the miniature Mt. Fuji in the center. The general plan of the garden is considered an attempt to reproduce in miniature the fifty-three stages on the old Tokaido highway, on which daimyo traveled to and from Edo.

34. *Back garden of private house.*

Tsubo Niwa ("Jar Gardens")

Tsubo niwa is the generic name applied to very small gardens located between buildings. The word *tsubo* has two possible derivations: one is from a unit of square measure (1 *tsubo* equals 3.3 square meters), and the other from a word of identical pronunciation that refers to a type of jar or pot. This latter word brings to mind the old Chinese legend of "the world in a jar," from which developed the Japanese phrase *kochu-no-ten* and its meaning of a life of contentment in a very small, secluded place.

The *tsubo niwa* at Ninna-ji (p. 52) lies between the Shinden Main Hall and the Kuro-shoin. It is nothing but a dozen small bamboo trees, a few stones and moss; so small and so ordinary that it would seem hardly to deserve the name of garden. But a careful and sensitive visitor may discover for himself some *raison d'être* for such a tiny place.

The Totekiko garden at Ryogen-in, Daitoku-ji compound (p. 53), is less than ten square meters in area, lying to the east of the Abbot's Chambers and bordered at the other end by the Living Quarters. The simple pattern of two rings of ripples around stones resembles the ripples made by dripping water [I, 152]. This is perhaps the apotheosis of Zen philosophy, "To see the whole universe in a garden-jar," or, as the English poet William Blake wrote, "To see the world in a grain of sand."

The garden at Tokai-an (p. 18) is another example of a *tsubo niwa*.

Fig. 34   The back garden of a private house is usually a *tsubo niwa*. It is there to be viewed from the living quarters, and it has been much influenced by the teahouse garden. An example is shown in Fig. 34. This type of garden is much to be valued now when houses are so densely packed together in Japan that there is hardly space for a proper garden.

Flowering Trees and Coloring Leaves

The most important materials of a garden are water, trees and stones. Then come moss, lawns, sand, and additional adornments. Trees must have been the first to be used when man started making gardens. Almost every kind of tree has been planted in gardens, but still there are conventions and traditions. Evergreen trees, particularly the pine (*matsu*) and the Japanese cypress (*hinoki*), are regarded as propitious and are usually planted at the focal point of the garden. The Horai-style garden, symbolizing the Islands of Eternal Youth, must always have a pine.

The dry landscape garden, which has been the predominant form of garden since the end of the Muromachi period, focuses on stone compositions, eschewing flowering trees. When trees are planted, they are usually evergreens, or evergreen shrubs that can be trimmed. The only exception are azaleas, because they can also be trimmed.

In teahouse gardens, flowering trees are not used, but instead grasses with flowers may be planted at the foot of some trees. There is, however, no rigid rule on these matters.

We say a garden "grows" as the trees grow, and there are attendant advantages and disadvantages. A technique employed to overcome the disadvantages is trimming, which will be illustrated under a different heading.

The double-blossomed cherry tree (*kokonoe-zakura*, "nine-folded cherry blossom") at Joshoko-ji (p. 54) is about five hundred years old, the oldest cherry tree in Kyoto. It is in front of a hall that is both the Buddhist Sanctum and Founder's Hall.

The garden at Chikurin-in in Nara Prefecture (p. 55), called Gunho-en, is a pond-garden for viewing from the building, and is attributed to Hosokawa Yusai. There are cherry trees and magnolias by the lake. Spring is the best season for visiting this temple.

The South Garden of the Main Hall at Koto-in, Daitoku-ji compound (p. 56), is full of maple trees, among which stands a solitary stone lantern. This temple abounds in maples, which

35. *Trimmed shrubs in garden of Main Hall, Daitoku-ji.*

of all trees displays the greatest variety throughout the year—especially notable are the fresh green leaves of May and the crimson leaves of autumn.

The garden at Mantoku-ji, Obama City in Fukui Prefecture (p. 57), has a maple tree more than three hundred years old and a dry landscape stone composition. The beauty of the old maple leaves is enhanced by the contrast with the evergreen pines and shrubs. This garden was made in the early Edo period.

The construction of the garden at Shozan (p. 58) began in 1955 and was completed recently. It is a very large garden full of variety. The photograph shows part of it, including a plum orchard. The three hills of Takagamine are used as background; one of them is seen here.

MATERIALS AND THE SENSE OF BEAUTY

The Rhythm of Trimming

Seasonal pruning is a commonplace operation performed yearly on all trees in a garden. Trimming (*karikomi*), on the other hand, is a drastic, selective device, the purpose of which is to preserve the original size and shape of trees so that the total effect of the garden is not changed. Trimming began to be used on a regular basis in the Momoyama period, and gardens with trimmed trees and shrubs as their main feature were laid out in the Edo period.

The device originated in the dry landscape garden that began under the influence of Zen culture in the Muromachi period.

36. *Garden of large trimmed shrubs at Daichi-ji.*

Its demand for a symbolic or abstract kind of representation extended to trees. Even the dry garden had to have some trees—the garden of Ryoan-ji is a rare exception—and the attitude towards trees underwent a revolutionary change through this new type of garden.

Trimming can be roughly divided into the large and the small type. Of the large trimming there are many kinds, such as single, double, and even three-fold hedge-trimming, wavy trimming, square and round trimming, and trimming in the shape *Fig. 35* of steps. The garden of the Main Hall at Daitoku-ji has large trimmed shrubs behind a dry waterfall composition, and the *Fig. 36* garden of Daichi-ji in Shiga Prefecture [I, 82] has large trimmed hedges that simulate the undulation of waves. The small type is the trimming of a single or a few trees or shrubs into round, square, or other shapes. These trees and shrubs may be arranged separately or in groups. The small type is appropriate to home gardens. For fine examples of trimming other than those mentioned above, see page eight (double-trimmed hedge), page twenty-five (small trimming), and page forty-six (long-trimmed hedge seen as triple when viewed from outside the garden).

The garden at Raikyu-ji, Takahashi City, Okayama Prefecture (p. 60), was built in 1600 by Kobori Enshu when he was a young man; it displays the early flowering of his genius. The trimmed hedge is the highlight of the garden.

In the garden at Shoden-ji, Kyoto (p. 61), trimmed shrubs are planted in an unusual "seven-five-three" arrangement on the white sand. This garden is attributed to Kobori Enshu, and its unique design and structure would appear to confirm this.

37. *Nachi Waterfall.*

38. *Greater Waterfall, Shugaku-in Imperial Villa.*

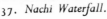

The Sound of Waterfalls and Streams

The relation between garden and water has been inseparable from the very beginning—ponds, waterfalls, streams, and fountains being utilized to impress not only the eye but also the ear. Since the sounds of running water cannot be reproduced in photographs, they must be imagined by the reader.

In days of old, people regarded waterfalls as incarnations of gods, and one of the ascetic exercises of certain Buddhist sects consisted in standing under a waterfall to be bathed in the falling water. The Nachi Waterfall in Wakayama Prefecture is one of the sites for such exercises, which are still practiced today.

Fig. 37

In Fig. 38 is shown a miniature waterfall at Shugaku-in Imperial Villa, the largest of several in the garden.

Fig. 38

When a dry garden was laid out, a dry waterfall, a dry pond, and a dry stream were represented by sand and stones, displaying the love of nature and especially the attachment to water in the Japanese mind. The most famous dry composition is that of Daisen-in (p. 14).

Fig. 39

The oldest surviving example of a waterfall composition is that of Nakoso-no-Taki at Daitoku-ji, in the *sanzon* style (p. 62). Originally there was running water, but, as is often mentioned in old *waka* poems, the waterfall long ago became dry.

39. Dry waterfall composition, Daisen-in.

There are two waterfalls, "male" and "female," in the garden at Erin-ji in Enzan City, Yamanashi Prefecture (p. 63). Muso was asked to be founder of the temple, and the garden is attributed to him. He seems to have attached much importance to waterfalls, for they are a feature of many gardens attributed to him, such as Saiho-ji [I, 66] and Tenryu-ji (p. 21). Erin-ji is well known as the temple of the Zen priest Kaisen, who, when Oda Nobunaga and his army attacked and set fire to the temple in 1582, said, "Clear your mind of all thoughts, and you will find even a burning fire cool," and threw himself into the fire, followed by a hundred of his disciples.

Sengetsusen at Jisho-ji (p. 64), Ginkaku-ji (Silver Pavilion), is a very small waterfall, but the old stone formation around it is impressive. The trickling sound can faintly be heard from the Devotional Hall (Togu-do).

The garden at Saimyo-ji in Shiga Prefecture (p. 65) has a *sanzon*-style dry waterfall composition on the upper part of the hill and a Yakushi-*sanzon* composition on the lower part; both are quite appropriate to a temple in a mountain district.

The three-level waterfall at Jakko-in (p. 66), half-hidden in the corner of the garden, has a certain feminine quality appropriate to a convent.

In the Heian period, water was led into the garden from any nearby river, and the murmur of a brook and sometimes the trickling of a mountain stream were reproduced in the garden. Using such streams, the graceful and elegant game of *kyokusui-no-en* was performed on the third of March. Each of the court nobles sitting along the stream would compose a *waka* poem be-

40. *Nara-no-Ogawa stream, Kamigamo Shrine.*　　　　41. *Nagare-no-Niwa, Ritsu-in.*

fore the wine cup that came from upstream reached and passed him; then he would drink the *sake* in the cup. The poems would be recited afterwards in the hall.

Fig. 40 Something of the old appearance of those streams is preserved in the stream called Nara-no-Ogawa at Kamigamo Shrine,
Fig. 41 Kyoto. Nagare-no-Niwa [I, 81], Ritsu-in, Shiga Prefecture, is an Edo version of the same tradition.

The Inner Garden at Kyoto Imperial Palace (p. 67) follows the taste and fashion of the Heian-period garden.

Of the gardens laid out during the Meiji and Taisho periods near Nanzen-ji in Kyoto, those at Murin-an, Tairyuzan-so, and Hekiun-so are the most representative. That of Murin-an is shown on page sixty-eight.

Just as there is a dry waterfall composition, so is there a dry stream composition. Typical examples are at Daisen-in [I, 48] and Shinnyo-in (detail on p. 16).

Bridges

In Japan, primitive bridges made of a single log or suspended by ivy and vines gradually developed into wooden bridges. In laying a bridge, two things must be taken into account: that is, the practical purpose of crossing over the river, and the harmony with the natural environment. Outstanding examples are Ujibashi, Karahashi at Seta, and Kintaibashi in Iwakuni.

There are, however, two types of garden bridge, one with a practical purpose and the other for aesthetic effect only. Earlier examples of bridges mostly belong to the latter kind;

42. *Stone Bridge in dry garden, Juko-in.*

43. *Bridge to the Tortoise Islet, Sambo-in.*

Fig. 42

Fig. 43

Fig. 44

the stone bridge at Tenryu-ji in front of the waterfall composition ([I, 60] and p. 21) is possibly one of them. Even those of later years, such as those at Ginkaku-ji (p. 70) and Chishaku-in [I, 14] are not built to be used; nor are those in dry gardens, such as those at Daisen-in (p. 14) and Juko-in.

The Islands of Eternal Youth and Immortality, and the Crane and Tortoise Islets, were originally meant only to be approached by boat and never intended to be trodden on, since they were regarded as sacred places. But with the passage of time, this religious implication disappeared and people began to lay bridges to them, as in the case of Sambo-in. At Katsura Imperial Villa, which was built after Sambo-in, the islands are free of any religious implication: they are there for the sake of beauty and for visiting across the bridges. At last, human interest has come to dominate over the religious.

Musaibashi Bridge at Eiho-ji, Tajimi City, Gifu Prefecture (p. 69), is placed at the focal point of the pond-garden. It is an old example of a bridge with a roofed resting-place in the middle. Chitosebashi in the Upper Garden of Shugaku-in Imperial Villa is in the same tradition.

The stone bridge at Ginkaku-ji (Silver Pavilion) (p. 70) is in front of the Devotional Hall (Togu-do). It is made of two natural stones, and the part of the garden around it is considered to be important because it is only here that the original form of the garden is still preserved intact.

The South Garden of Sento Imperial Palace was laid out by Kobori Enshu in 1634. The former wooden bridge, called Eight Bridges (Yatsuhashi), was replaced by a stone one in 1895, and

44. *Bridge, Shugaku-in Imperial Villa.*

it has a wisteria arbor which is very beautiful when in full blossom (p. 71).

Genkyu-en in Hikone City, Shiga Prefecture (p. 72), is a daimyo garden built in 1679, but the stone composition of the island suggests earlier construction, possibly in the Momoyama period. The general plan of the garden is possibly an attempt at reproducing the Eight Scenic Views around Lake Biwa. If so, the wooden bridge to the right represents Karahashi Bridge at Seta.

Shukkei-en in Hiroshima City (p. 73) is an equally fine example of a daimyo garden. It was laid out around 1620, but has been remodeled many times since then, most recently following the damage caused during World War II. A stone bridge and an earthen bridge display fine balance and contrast. What is called an earthen bridge is in fact a wooden bridge covered with an earth casing.

The stone bridge in the dry garden at the Former Senshu-kaku Pavilion, Tokushima Castle (p. 74), is the longest bridge of natural stone to be found in a dry garden.

Stepping-Stones, Pavements, and Paths

Except for gardens laid out before the Muromachi period, almost all gardens we see today have stepping-stones and pavements. The use of the stepping-stone (*tobiishi*) originated with

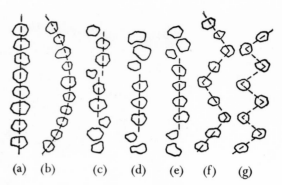

45. *Some examples of stepping-stone patterns:* (a)*straight,*
(b) *large curve,* (c) *two-in-a-line,* (d) *three-in-a-line,*
(e) *four-in-a-line,* (f) *large zigzag,* (g) *small zigzag.*

the tea-master Sen-no-Rikyu, to allow guests to walk along the path to the teahouse without getting their straw sandals wet. Rikyu said, "Stepping-stones are sixty percent practical and forty percent beauty." But his disciple, Furuta Oribe, said that they are "forty percent practical and sixty percent beauty." This difference of opinion may be due to the different styles of teahouses and paths they constructed: Rikyu's hut style and Oribe's study-hall (*shoin*) style. Rikyu used rather small stones while Oribe preferred larger ones. In later years many principles for laying stones were formulated, and some examples are here shown. Rikyu himself was not dogmatic but stressed the *Fig. 45* harmonious fusion of practicality and beauty.

The stones used are natural and hewn ones. Sometimes stones from famous old monasteries or from stone mills were also used. The device of stepping-stones thus originated in the teahouse garden and later was introduced to other types of gardens, especially daimyo gardens, where they were used in the construction of paths for strolling. The best example of the latter type of garden is that of Katsura Imperial Villa.

There are three kinds of pavement (*shikiishi*) generally placed at the entrance or near the buildings. The first is a pavement of hewn stones of square, diagonal, or other shape, its effect being the most formal of the three types of pavement. Shown here are the *shikiishi* of Tenju-an and the *shikiishi* of Katsura Imperial *Fig. 46* Villa, consisting of a view of the Inner Gate and the pavement *Fig. 47* from the Carriage Approach, facing the opposite direction of the view on page seventy-eight. The second kind is made of natural stones of various shapes. Sometimes hewn stones are

46. *Stone pavement, Tenju-an.*   47. *Stone pavement and Inner Gate, Katsura Imperial Villa.*

mixed with them. The effect of this type is semiformal, the joints being irregular and uneven. The last kind consists of naturally round stones, the flat parts of which lie uppermost. *Nobedan* is the word used for a stretch of the third type of pavement, the most informal of the three, conveying an atmosphere of rural beauty.

At Saiho-ji (Moss Temple), after passing through the gate that separates the Upper Garden from the Lower Garden, the visitor climbs a flight of informally laid stone steps. Due to the fact that the stones are arranged exactly like stepping-stones (except for the differences in height between steps), they are known as the stepping-stone steps (p. 75).

The back approach to Kozan-ji in Kyoto is covered with fallen leaves in late autumn as is shown on page seventy-six.

The pavement of Shinju-an, Daitoku-ji compound (p. 77), leads one from the gate to the Inner Gate (center) and to the entrance (to the right before the Inner Gate, not shown here). The graceful composition of the pine trees matches the formal atmosphere of the pavement.

The pavement that extends from the gate to the Carriage Approach of Katsura Imperial Villa is called the "True Pavement" (*shin-no-shikiishi*) (p. 78). Its rigidity is relieved by the natural stones laid on both sides. At the other end of the pave-

48. *Lane of pines connecting gardens, Shugaku-in Imperial Villa.*

49. *Stepping-stones in pond, Shokuho-en.*

ment, there are five square stepping-stones placed near the gate. It is a rare and fine achievement.

The stepping-stones laid in a straight line (p. 79) produce a beautiful composition with the straight line of bricks embroidering the lawn. Small pebbles are laid between larger stones in tracks around the buildings; they absorb water and prevent the rain dropping from the eaves from wearing a channel in the ground.

The byway of white sand in the Lower Garden of Shugaku-in Imperial Villa (p. 80, above) may be considered the prelude to the other gardens at Shugaku-in.

In the pavement of the Rin'un-tei Summerhouse, in the Upper Garden, are set black pebbles—either singly or in clusters of two or three, hence their name "one-two-three stones" (p. 80, below). Just in front of the rectangular convex stone step are set two thick black square tiles.

The landing-place in the Upper Garden (p. 81) is made of two stone steps, and there is a third stone like a column, which was probably used for securing the boat. The landing-place at Katsura Imperial Villa is provided with stone lanterns (cf. p. 109, above), but here in the Upper Garden we have none. It may be that this summerhouse was used only as a daytime resting-place.

Fig. 48   At Shugaku-in there runs, among rice fields, a lane bordered by pine trees. From here there is a splendid view of nearby Mt. Hiei, whose appearance alters according to the time of day and season. The ex-Emperor Gomizunoö first made the lane

50. *Black sand in Ryogin-an garden.*

when he constructed the villa, using the original footpaths between the rice fields, thereby not disturbing the farmers whom he wished to observe at close hand.

The path of the Ura Senke School (p. 82), running laterally from the "Helmet Gate" (*Kabuto Mon*), is called a "hailstone" pavement. In teahouse gardens the approach from the gate to the house entrance is very important and, as can be seen here, great care has been taken in its arrangement. For the pine leaves beside the pavement, see page 110.

Across the Blue-Dragon Lake at the Heian Shrine are stepping-stones (*sawatari*) made from pieces of the old Sanjo Bridge. Collectively, these stepping-stones are generally called the Reclining Dragon Bridge.

Fig. 49   The *sawatari* at Hakusa Sonso Villa has a bamboo railing [I, 25], and that at Shokuho-en is an example of a happy combination of practicality and beauty.

Sand Patterns

Sand not only makes the surface of the earth beautiful, but also has an important function as a garden material. The true merit of sand was clearly shown by the appearance of the dry landscape garden, in which water was replaced by sand.

Fig. 50   The sand used in gardens is usually white, but there are some exceptions. The garden of Ryogin-an, Tofuku-ji compound, uses black sand representing black clouds. There are allusions in old books that the garden of Kinkaku-ji (Golden Pavilion) once had sand of five colors.

51. *Examples of water and checkered sand patterns.*

Fig. 51   Patterns are always drawn in the sand of dry gardens, ranging from the simple to the complex ones shown here. They represent the ocean, a river, a stream, a ripple, and so on, and enable us to appreciate the beauty of sand even more deeply.

White sand is not only spread flat but is sometimes shaped into a mound. In front of the Main Hall of Ginkaku-ji there is a sand composition supposedly symbolizing the West Lake (Si-hu) in China. The sand is here spread in a fan-like shape and is about one meter high. There is a pattern on the sand consisting of over a dozen stripes.

Fig. 52   There is also a mound of sand nearby in the shape of a truncated cone, about two meters high, symbolizing perhaps a pavilion by the lakeside. The exact date and the intention of the layout of these rather amazing compositions are unknown. It is generally believed, however, that they were made after the middle of the Edo period [I, 134]. These compositions of rare originality give an unexpected effect on a moon-lit night by seeming to reflect the moonlight.

The mounds of sand may originate from those in the gardens of Zen temples. The South Garden of the Abbot's Hall at Daisen-in (p. 85) was originally a place for ceremonial performances and had no stone composition or trimmed shrubs. Later, only the line-patterns in the sand and the two sand mounds were added. Thus, a representative garden of the Muromachi period was preserved even after ceremonies had begun to be performed indoors and its functional purpose had been lost.

White sand with a sea-design is always beautiful to the eye,

52. Sand mound, Ginkaku-ji
(Silver Pavilion).

but the checkered pattern shown on page eighty-six has an incomparable effect. This garden, in front of the Founder's Hall at Tofuku-ji, with a checkered pattern in the foreground and trimmed shrubs behind it, is a peculiar combination of two kinds of Japanese garden, the Zen and *shoin* styles (cf. p. 89).

The garden at Bairin-in, Kurume City, Fukuoka Prefecture (p. 87), belongs to the Myoshin-ji School of Zen, and is one of the largest in West Japan. The place has a quiet atmosphere appropriate to religious training.

The garden of Kishiwada Castle, Osaka Prefecture (p. 88), was made by Shigemori Mirei in 1953. The garden has been constructed so that it can be properly viewed from the castle donjon. The eight groups of stone compositions, placed on the wave-pattern of white sand, show a very modern sensitivity.

Moss and Lawns

The function of moss in the garden is to delight the eye. It is difficult to know exactly when it was introduced into the garden, but it seems to have attracted attention as early as the Heian period, and its beauty was recognized during the Kamakura and Muromachi periods. When the teahouse garden was

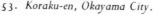

53. *Koraku-en, Okayama City.* 54. *Moss-and-sand garden, Obai-in, Daitoku-ji compound.*

created in the Momoyama period, moss came to be much appreciated, and throughout the Edo period it was used in all kinds of gardens.

Many people think that the introduction of the lawn into the garden is the result of western influence, but actually it has long been used in Japan for both practical and aesthetic reasons. Rikyu used a lawn for the path to the teahouse, but later used moss, which was in turn replaced by stepping-stones. The lawn is more suitable to a large space rather than a small patch of garden. Thus, in the daimyo gardens built during the Edo *Fig. 53* period it was used extensively. For examples see Koraku-en in Okayama City, Rikugi-en in Tokyo [I, 108], Joju-en at Suizen-ji (p. 51), Ritsurin Park ([I, 96]; and p. 9), Genkyu-en in Shiga (p. 72), and Joei-ji (p. 24).

Tofuku-ji compound (p. 89) is said to have been built by the painter Sesshu. It was left in ruins for many years until restored by Mr. Shigemori in 1949, and repaired again by Mr. Nakane in 1957. The garden is divided into two parts, one with only white sand and the other with moss, trees, and stones. The *Fig. 54* same technique is employed in the garden of Obai-in, Daitoku-ji compound.

Some visitors are pleasantly surprised by the Moss Garden at Heisen-ji, in Katsuyama City, Fukui Prefecture (p. 90), for it possesses an atmosphere even more natural than that of the Moss Temple in Kyoto.

Shuko-en, attached to the Iizuka residence, Kashiwazaki City, Niigata Prefecture (p. 91), is a pond-garden for strolling, built at the end of the Edo period. The stepping-stones in the pond (*sawatari*), with moss and pine leaves scattered on top, resemble Japanese cakes.

The garden at Gio-ji in Kyoto (p. 92) has so tender an atmosphere that it is loved by everyone, young and old. In the first volume is a scene of autumnal leaves [I, 63], and here we have fresh maple leaves.

The patterns of moss seen in the white sand at Sambo-in (p. 93, above) represent a gourd and cup. It is said that the abbot made it during the Taisho period in commemoration of the famous flower-viewing visit of Toyotomi Hideyoshi in 1598. The designer possessed both taste and a sense of humor.

The pattern of moss at Rozan-ji (p. 93, below) copies that of clouds often found in the picture scrolls of the Heian period. It is quite appropriate to this temple, for it has recently been proved that this is where Lady Murasaki, the authoress of *The Tale of Genji*, had her house. The broad bell flowers (*kikyo*) that grow out of the moss add to the charm.

The dry garden at Saiko-ji in Uwajima City, Ehime Prefecture (p. 94), was made in 1625, and the lawn is planted along the dry stream. The stone composition, dry pond, and the trimmed hedges and shrubs together produce an excellent effect.

The pond-garden at the Jonan-gu Shrine is shown in the first volume [I, 70]. Here is the dry garden (p. 95), with its somewhat tropical atmosphere. The lawn extends to the stone composition, cycads, and large trimmed trees behind.

Fences and Gates

Fences, or walls, and gates either border the garden or are placed inside it. The styles and forms vary a great deal, and the name of the temple that uses a particular style is usually given to the style. Thus there are styles of fences or walls named after those at Kennin-ji, Daitoku-ji, Kinkaku-ji, Ginkaku-ji, Ryoan-ji, Koho-an, Koetsu-ji, so on. As elsewhere, practicality is united harmoniously with visual appeal.

On entering the gate of Ginkaku-ji (Silver Pavilion), one will find a simple bamboo fence one meter high on a low stone wall (the most common form of the Kennin-ji fence) with the addition of a hedge behind the fence (p. 96). This three-storied fence is called the Ginkaku-ji fence. On the opposite side of the path, there are what may be called "two-storied hedges"

55. Double hedge at Daisen-in.

56. Fence, Koho-an, Daitoku-ji compound.

57. Katsura fence and bamboo hedge, Katsura Imperial Villa.

58. Inner Gate, Enri-an.

of camellias and other trees, showing a marked contrast with the fence.

Fig. 55   Hedges, as has been said in reference to trimming, add accent to the scene, an example being the double hedge of Daisen-in (p. 85).

Fig. 56   The fence at Koho-an, Daitoku-ji compound, shows a stable balance by the use of thick bamboo stems crossed in a rhomboid shape.

Fig. 57   The Katsura hedge at Katsura Imperial Villa (p. 97) has classical features. It is connected at the end with a hedge of bamboo trees, a unique arrangement.

The roof of the Baiken-mon gate, an inner gate of the Omote Senke School (p. 98), is thatched with cedar bark kept in place by split bamboo. The door leaves and wings are of bamboo

59. *Flanking fence, Shisen-do.*

stalks placed at intervals so that one may catch a glimpse of the beautiful interior. The stepping-stones lead one through the gate of the path to the Fushin-an Teahouse.

There are beautiful gates of many varieties on the paths of all three Senke schools; the *nakakuguri* of the Omote Senke School [I, 44] is perhaps one of the most unusual.

Koetsu-ji has a fence that bears its name, and of which the photograph (p. 99) shows a section. The fence extends in a semicircle, its height gradually decreasing from one end to the other. The plant in blossom is bush clover.

In the north corner of the South Garden at Keishun-in, Myoshin-ji compound, there are hedges and an inner gate that leads to the teahouse (p. 100). The Myoshin-ji School of Zen, unlike the Daitoku-ji School, rejects the tea ceremony, and the teahouse is concealed in a corner of the garden. Thus, even the Inner Gate shows a touch of reserve. It is interesting to compare it with the Inner Gate of the Kiyomizu Rokubei Villa (p. 101).

Fig. 58 The Inner Gate of Enri-an, Kyoto, is unique in that it has a resting-place attached to it.

Fig. 59 The flanking fence (*sodegaki*) of Shisen-do has a poetic quality enhanced by the addition of flowering grasses. A flanking fence is placed at a certain part of the garden to screen the view as well as to add flavor to the scene.

157

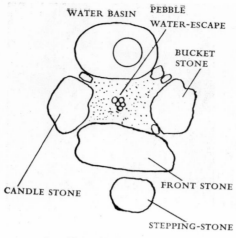

60. *Water-basin and stone composition.*

61. *Water basin in stream, Hakusa Sonso.*

Water Basins

Fig. 60

The stone water basin usually found at the approach to a shrine is there to enable the visitor to cleanse his mouth and wash his hands, as a symbolic act of purification. The water basin was introduced into the teahouse garden during the Momoyama period, together with the device of stepping-stones and other features. Later, it came to be used in almost all gardens. The name *tsukubai* comes from the movement of crouching towards the basin when washing one's hands.

The basin is made of natural stone, hewn stone, or sometimes stonework recast into a basin. The shapes vary a great deal, and the famous and historic basins are preserved by well-known families and various temples.

The basin in front of the Yuin Teahouse (p. 102) is made of an old stone formerly used at a pagoda. It has a Buddha in relief on each of the four sides.

There are two famous basins at Koho-an, Daitoku-ji compound. Shown here is the one in front of the San'unjo Teahouse (p. 103). It is in the shape of an old coin with two Chinese characters in relief. The other famous basin is in front of the Bosen Tearoom.

Ryoan-ji has a water basin traditionally believed to be the gift of Mito Mitsukuni, with four Chinese characters in relief

62, 63. *Stone lanterns of Nanso-ji* (left) *and of Katsura Imperial Villa* (right).

meaning "I know only that I am content" (p. 104). In each of the four characters is a small "square" (吾 唯 知 足) which is beautifully and wittily represented in the design of the basin by the square cavity in the center.

The basin in Manshu-in (p. 105) has a birdlike figure, possibly that of an owl, on each of the four sides.

The basin of Ni-no-Maru in Nagoya Castle (p. 106) is made of a natural stone with a long oval cavity on the flat side. The imposing shape of this basin is appropriate to the site.

In Katsura Imperial Villa, the stream by the Shokin-tei Teahouse provides a unique example of a washing-place without a basin (p. 107).

Fig. 61   At the Hakusa Sonso Villa, the basin is found located in the waters of the stream.

Stone Lanterns

Stone lanterns, like water basins, were originally placed at shrines and only later introduced into the teahouse garden. Rikyu seems to have taken a fancy to a stone lantern when he was walking around Toribeno, a graveyard in east Kyoto, for they were dedicated to graveyards as well as to temples and shrines. Generally speaking, old and moss-covered lanterns were sought out for placing beside paths.

Fig. 62
Fig. 63   Harmony with the surroundings must be the most important factor in deciding which of the many kinds of lanterns to choose. Those at Katsura Imperial Villa are excellent: they are

64, 65. *Stone lantern in front of Hoö-do* (left) *and "stone pennant" at Hakusa Sonso* (right).

possibly the best models to imitate or ponder upon when seeking to understand lanterns.

The lantern at Ryogen-in, Daitoku-ji compound (p. 108), with a chrysanthemum crest on its cap, was recently dedicated to the memory of Shinzen, the founder of the temple. To the left there is an old sasanqua tree, to which is given the name of Yokihi (Yang Kuei Fei), the beautiful Chinese imperial consort of the T'ang dynasty, who is often compared to Cleopatra.

There are more than twenty lanterns of different shapes at Katsura Imperial Villa. The lantern shown on page 109 (top) stands by the landing-place for the Shoiken Teahouse, and has a most unusual and fascinating shape. It is low, but can still illuminate the waterside. One side is carved in the shape of the sun and moon, while the others are carved as stars; hence its name, "stone lantern of three lights."

The Oribe-style lantern on the path to the San'unjo Teahouse at Koho-an (p. 109, below) has the shape of a cross with a relief of the Virgin Mary at its front. It is generally called the Christian Stone Lantern.

Figs. 64, 65   Lanterns of other shapes are also shown here.

Other Adornments

Pine needles are spread over the moss during winter at the Ura Senke School as protection against frost and snow (p. 110).

In Kenroku-en Park, Kanazawa City, Ishikawa Prefecture, we find a unique device for protecting pine branches from breaking under the pressure of heavy snow (p. 111). One end of a length of rope is tied to a branch and the other end to a pole protruding above the tree. The tying of many ropes in this manner produces a Japanese umbrellalike shape in which the ropes are the ribs. The quivering of the ropes under pressure shakes the snow off the branches.

At Shisen-do the water of the stream running through the lower part of the garden is caught by a small hinged pipe of bamboo, one end of which is thrown back onto a stone whenever the balance is upset by the weight of the water (p. 112). The regular sound of bamboo striking stone was originally used to frighten away marauding wild boars; hence the name *shishi-odoshi* (boar frightener). With time it lost its practical use and became an adornment.

The reader interested in garden terms should consult the Glossary at the end of *Invitation to Japanese Gardens*.

Alphabetical List of Gardens

The numbers on the right refer to page numbers of plates. Macrons are given in garden names at left only.